WEYMOUTH
The Golden Years

WEYMOUTH

The Golden Years

PHOTOGRAPHS BY GRAHAM HERBERT

INTRODUCTION & CAPTIONS BY MAUREEN ATTWOOLL

DORSET BOOKS

First published in 2001 by Dorset Books
Reprinted in 2001, 2002

ISBN 1 871164 37 0

British Library Cataloguing-in-Publication-Data
A CIP data for this book is available from the British Library

DORSET BOOKS
Official publisher to Dorset County Council
Halsgrove House
Lower Moor Way
Tiverton EX16 6SS
T: 01884 243242
F: 01884 243325
www.halsgrove.com

Printed and bound in Great Britain by Bookcraft, Midsomer Norton

CONTENTS

ACKNOWLEDGEMENTS

My task of selecting illustrations from the Herbert negatives was made infinitely easier due to the comprehensive and very detailed index to the negatives compiled, in his retirement, by Jack West, former Chief Librarian and Museum Curator of Weymouth and my thanks go first and foremost to him.

Brian Jackson, transport historian, helped me to select the harbour pictures and possesses the most amazing memory of local events.

Ruth Lawrence, Graham Herbert's daughter, was kind enough to supply me with details of the career of her late father.

Profolab of Weymouth produced the excellent prints from the negatives.

Sue Wright deciphered my handwriting and put the text onto disk.

Dorset Books and Dorset County Library encouraged me to undertake the project.

To all of them, my grateful thanks – and to my husband David, whose life and home have once more been taken over by 'local history'.

INTRODUCTION

All the photographs in this book were taken by one man - professional photographer Graham Valentine Herbert, A.I.B.P., A.R.P.S. Graham Herbert's family moved to Weymouth in the 1920s. His father, S.J.Herbert set up a photographic business in the town, in which he was joined by his two sons Graham and Donald and their sister Gladys. Donald later moved to Southampton and on his father's death Graham took over the family business, operating from a shop, 'Herbert of Weymouth', in St Thomas Street, and latterly from his home in Dorchester Road.

On Graham Herbert's death in 1983, his widow Mollie presented his large collection of photographic negatives to Weymouth Library. He had worked all over Dorset but particularly in Weymouth and Portland and it is from the Weymouth negatives that this selection has been made, with an occasional view from farther afield for an event of general local interest.

Just a few of the photographs date from the 1930s, but the majority date from the 1950s to early 1980s. There are none of the war years when Graham Herbert volunteered for the RAF, working in the photographic section in Italy and North Africa. Many photographs are from the Fifties when family albums were filled with tiny black and white snapshots, but few were recording the local scene in such detail as this.

As a seaside resort Weymouth was well and truly back in business at the end of the Second World War. After years of travel restrictions, rationing and shortages of almost everything there was renewed demand for the family holiday by the sea, which varied little from those of the Twenties and Thirties – sun, sand, sea and 'B & B'. The era of cheap air fares and package tours abroad was still a few years in the future.

Weymouth is fortunate that its elegant Esplanade buildings remain almost unspoiled. They have overlooked countless thousands of holidaymakers on the beach since the days when King George III brought the town fame as royalty's favourite health and pleasure resort. The harbourside provides picturesque and ever-changing scenes. Photographs of the town centre will evoke memories of shops and businesses long gone. Some changes pass almost unnoticed – a new shopfront here, a building replaced there. Occasionally a whole street makes way for redevelopment – or car parking. The post-war boom in car sales is very evident in some of these traffic-clogged scenes.

Certainly, not all the scenes are attractively nostalgic. Enemy air raids destroyed much of old Weymouth on the south side of the harbour where bomb-scarred streets of ruined and boarded-up houses were to remain until the early 1960s.

The pre-war landscape of rural areas outside the town changed almost unrecognisably as housing needs were met. Large estates took over green fields at Wyke, Westham and Littlemoor and new houses at Southill and Preston expanded those communities dramatically. Some grand mansions of an earlier age were bulldozed, developers building several dozen homes on what had previously been the extensive gardens of just one family.

It is perhaps easy to look at these pictures of how things were and think 'If only...' but towns cannot stand still and their inhabitants have changing needs.

Change, celebration and the occasional disaster are all recorded through Graham Herbert's camera lens. A little historical detail has been added to each photograph to 'set the scene'.

BUS

CHAPTER ONE

SPECIAL OCCASIONS

Royal occasions, celebrations, sports events and jubilations

On 8 February 1952, surrounded by a crowd of some 2000 strong, the Mayor, Alderman H.A. Medlam reads the proclamation of the accession of Queen Elizabeth II. Overlooking the seafront scene is the statue of King George III, the new Queen's great-great-great-great grandfather.

Television sets were still a luxury item in the early 1950s, but sales increased in 1953 when it became known that Queen Elizabeth II's Coronation was to be televised live from Westminster Abbey. Friends and neighbours gathered round (very) small screens to view the historic proceedings. Those who missed the grainy black and white TV showing were able to visit the Belle Vue Cinema the following month to watch the film 'A Queen is Crowned' in Technicolor. Here, members of the 3rd Wyke Regis Sea Scouts collect the film, suitably crowned, from Weymouth Railway Station. Unfortunately the only member of this cheery group to get his name in the local paper was 'Scamp', the scouts' doggy mascot!

The Coronation was celebrated by an abundance of street parties in the borough plus some more lasting memorials. Broadwey and Bincombe's contribution to the festivities was the installation of a seat at the junction of Dorchester Road and Weyview Crescent, unveiled by Alderman Medlam in November 1953.

Four ladies of the parish take the weight off their feet.

The new royal yacht *Britannia* was on her final trials at Portland in February 1954. The first of her 'royal' voyages took place later that year when she sailed from Portsmouth taking the young Prince Charles and Princess Anne to meet their parents (on a Commonwealth tour) at Tobruk. The Queen's floating home (it could be converted to a hospital ship in time of war) was decommissioned in December 1997 and the decision was made not to replace her. *Britannia* is now on permanent display at the Scottish port of Leith.

A four-hour inspection of H.M.S. *Eagle* on 29 April 1959 was Her Majesty the Queen's first visit to Weymouth and Portland since her accession to the throne in 1952. She arrived at Weymouth in the Royal Train and was driven along Weymouth Esplanade to the quay where the Royal Barge waited to take her to the aircraft carrier in the bay. The Queen, as Princess Elizabeth, had launched H.M.S. *Eagle* in 1946. It had not been announced that she would be accompanied by ten-year-old Prince Charles – a last-minute surprise which delighted the thousands-strong crowd thronging the Esplanade. Here, Lord Digby, Lord Lieutenant of Dorset, presents the Queen (hidden) and Prince Charles to the Royal Navy's Flag Officer Sea Training and Flag Officer Aircraft Carriers.

The Queen waves as the Royal Barge prepares to leave Weymouth Harbour.

The Barge sails out of Weymouth Harbour to H.M.S. *Eagle* in the Bay, accompanied by naval vessels and a 21-gun salute. The royal visitors later landed at Portland where they boarded the waiting Royal Train for the journey back to Windsor.

Admiral of the Fleet His Royal Highness the Duke of Edinburgh spent a day in Dorset in April 1955, visiting Portland in the morning and a sea training school at Parkstone later in the day. After meeting local dignitaries, the Duke inspected the Royal Guard provided by H.M.S. *Osprey* and the Sea Cadet Guard.

Tours of the Gunnery School and the Underwater Defence Establishment at Southwell were followed by lunch after which the Duke took off in the waiting Westland Sikorski helicopter for Parkstone.

In 1951 the Festival of Britain opened in London on the south bank of the Thames, a celebration aimed at raising people's spirits after years of war and hardship. Up river at Battersea were the Festival's Pleasure Gardens where the whimsical Guinness Clock was one of the attractions. Every quarter of an hour the Guinness man appeared, to ring his bell and announce a succession of feats of mechanical ingenuity. The clock came to Weymouth in the summer of 1953 and is shown here shortly after its installation in the Alexandra Gardens.

A poignant naval occasion in 1956. On 4 July 1940, sixteen years earlier to the day in Portland Harbour, H.M.S. *Foylebank* was attacked in a vicious Second World War air raid by German Junkers dive bombers. Leading Seaman Jack Mantle was manning the ship's starboard pom-pom during the attack. His left leg was shattered early in the raid but Jack Mantle stayed at his post, firing at the enemy aircraft until he fell, mortally wounded, beside his gun. For his gallantry in this action which sank his ship, Jack Mantle was posthumously awarded the Victoria Cross. In 1956, in his memory, this sun lounge was erected in the grounds of Portland Royal Naval Hospital. It was designed to resemble the bridge of a ship.

A sea cadet bugler from the Weymouth and Portland unit sounded Last Post and Reveille at the opening ceremony.

The lounge was opened by the Commander-in-Chief, Portsmouth, Admiral of the Fleet Sir George Creasy, seen here inviting Mr and Mrs Mantle, the naval hero's parents, to view the new building. In the 1980s the memorial began to show serious structural defects due to subsidence and had to be removed. Portland Naval Hospital, long transferred to civilian use, has also been partially demolished.

Some 30 U.S. Navy ships made an official visit to Portland in October 1957 following 'Strike Back', a ten-day Nato exercise. Focus of attention was on U.S.S. *Nautilus*, the world's first atomic-powered submarine, built at a cost of $40 million.

Nautilus was back at Portland and making world-wide headline news in August 1958. She was at the end of an epic pioneering voyage which had taken her under the Polar ice-cap – being submerged for ninety-six hours and covering a total of 1830 miles under the ice. Portland was her first port of call since leaving Honolulu three weeks earlier. Thousands gathered to welcome the submarine and a hectic week of celebrations and civic functions awaited her commander and crew.

U.S.S. *Skate* was the second atomic submarine to cross the North Pole under the ice, shortly after *Nautilus* in 1958. Skate had been at Portland in March that year having set a record of her own – the submarine had crossed the Atlantic in a new faster time of eight days and eleven hours, all submerged.

A seasonal visitor but there was no reindeer-drawn sleigh for Father Christmas when he journeyed to Weymouth in 1953. A Bere Regis coach brought him to the Bon Marche store in St Thomas Street, but his arrival was nonetheless an exciting event for the crowds of waiting children.

In 1958 Weymouth hosted an area heat of the 'National Lorry Driver of the Year' competition. Entrants assembled on the car park at the end of Westwey Road. Behind them loom the tall buildings of Weymouth Gasworks, none of which remain today. The site is now occupied by the D.S.S. building Westwey House which opened in 1972.

In modern times the granting of the 'Freedom of the Borough' dates from an 1850 Act of Parliament which enabled municipal corporations to confer the freedom on 'persons of distinction'. Percy Smallman, retiring Town Clerk of Weymouth and Melcombe Regis became a Freeman in 1956 having served the borough in that office for thirty years.

1959 saw the Freedom awarded to nuclear physicist Donald Fry, then deputy director of Harwell Atomic Energy Establishment whose appointment as head of the new Winfrith A.E.E. was announced on the day he became a Freeman of Weymouth. The photograph shows Sir John Cockcroft (right) congratulating Mr Fry. His wife, Mrs Jessie Fry (centre) was elected Mayor of Weymouth in 1978 and son Peter (admiring the scroll) is now the author of sporting books.

170 guests attended 'the biggest ever dinner held at the Royal Hotel' for Percy Smallman in 1956 and one wonders how those serving the food managed to struggle through such a tightly packed throng!

On a rain-soaked Esplanade on 22 October 1966 Mayor Lucie Hill conferred the Freedom of the Borough on 'R' Battery of the 250 (Queen's Own Dorset and West Somerset Yeomanry) Medium Regiment, Royal Artillery. The T.A. battery, based at Bincleaves Barracks, could now 'enter and march through the Borough on all ceremonial occasions with their guns and with their band playing.'

On the stage of the Alexandra Gardens Theatre, in front of the Union Jack and Tricolour, the official twinning ceremony between Louviers, France and Weymouth, England took place on 4 April 1959. French-born Mrs Iseult Legh, Mayor of Weymouth translated the proceedings for Monsieur Vincent, the Mayor of Louviers. Forty-plus years on the Weymouth Louviers Society is still going strong with frequent exchange visits between the two towns. Weymouth is also twinned with the German town of Holzewickede.

The Rotary Club of Weymouth had been fundraising since 1952 in the hope of opening the town's first community centre for older residents. The original aim had been to purchase and convert the Tudor House, No. 4 North Quay, but this building was demolished, after much controversy, in 1961. The centre opened at 'Pilgrim House' (originally known as the 'White House') in Hope Street in September 1962, where these ladies await the arrival of the Mayor for the official opening ceremony.

The most beautiful girl in the world… Twenty-one-year-old Lesley Langley of Preston, Weymouth won the 'Miss World' title in November 1965. She was welcomed home in January 1966 with a civic reception at the Pavilion Theatre. Here, the Mayor, Alderman Charles Armstrong, escorts her into the Gloucester Hotel for the lunch which followed.

1965 was centenary year for the Weymouth and Portland Railway but the anniversary excursion pictured here was tinged with regret. The line had closed to passengers in 1952 but continued in use for goods traffic until final closure in 1965. On 27 March three packed trains took 1000 passengers from Melcombe Regis Station to Easton, Portland for a final farewell. Loco 41324 has crossed the iron girder bridge and is approaching Littlefield Crossing, Abbotsbury Road. The lines have since been taken up and the old railway route is now a footpath from Westham to Wyke Regis, its walkers passing the overgrown platforms of the old halts along the way.

On the right is the subway for pedestrians – at least one impatient local motorist had been prosecuted for driving his car under here when a train was due!

The return journey, Westham Halt. This time the excursion train is pulled by loco 41284.

Weymouth's non-league 'Terras' made numerous post-war appearances in the early rounds of the F.A. Cup. Most notable were those of the 1949/50 season when the team reached the Third Round – losing to First Division Manchester United 4-0 at Old Trafford, and 1961/2 when Weymouth reached the Fourth Round to be beaten 2-0 in an away game by 2nd Division Preston North End. The photograph is of the 1967/68 season when Weymouth drew a First Round home game against Third Division Leyton Orient. Orient won 2-0 on a snowy ice-bound Rec. The football ground in Newstead Road relocated to Southill in the 1980s.

More than 40 powerboats roared past this vantage point at Portland Bill during the 12th International Offshore Power-boat Race in September 1972. Spectator numbers were down on previous years, possibly due to television coverage of that year's Olympic Games.

CHAPTER TWO

DISASTER!

Fire, flood, snow and shipwreck

The stranding of the 20 000-ton luxury Union Castle liner *Winchester Castle* on the night of 16 February 1936 provided Graham Herbert with a real scoop – this was the only photograph taken during the ship's brief stay on the rocks of Portland and it appeared in the national and local press. The *Winchester Castle* remained fast for some three hours below Blacknor, a spectacular sight, ablaze with lights from stern to stern. She slipped off on the rising tide and although slightly damaged was able to resume her voyage from Capetown to Southampton later the same day. There were no casualties among the crew and 338 passengers.

A long history of flooding and shingle deposits caused the all too frequent closure of Preston Beach Road. Damage following gales in November 1954 is shown here. The old sea wall and unsightly groynes were largely unsuccessful in curbing the power of the waves. It was not until 1995/6 that a huge new scheme of defence works was completed. The beach size was increased with more than 200,000 cubic metres of imported shingle and a rock groyne was added at the Weymouth end. At the same time a wide promenade was built along the new wall and there is now an uninterrupted walk along the Esplanade from Weymouth Pier to Overcombe.

Stranded! A typical scene on Preston Beach Road – these floods were in 1965.

'The Ritz is on fire!' – and practically every child on Easter holiday from school heard the news and rushed to Weymouth to join hundreds already watching the destruction of the Edwardian building. Opened in 1908 as 'The Pavilion' it was a real seaside confection of a pier theatre and a great loss to the Esplanade scene. Refurbishment for the summer season was under way when a painter's blowlamp set the largely wooden structure alight. The present Pavilion Theatre opened in 1960 on the same site.

Crowds gather in front of the blazing theatre.

Viewed across the harbour from Nothe Parade.

The devastated building. Lengthy litigation regarding the cause of the fire and compensation for the lessees of the theatre followed and there was much debate regarding the Ritz's replacement before the present Pavilion Theatre eventually opened six years after the conflagration.

The alarm was raised in May 1954 when contact was lost with the British 'S' class submarine *Scorcher*, exercising off Portland Bill. An immediate rescue drill was put into effect but the submarine, carrying a crew of 44 surfaced safely after two and a half hours unaware that as well as a communications failure, her marker buoy had been severed. *Scorcher* is seen here with the submarine depot ship H.M.S. *Maidstone*, a familiar sight at Portland in the 1950s.

The following year there was a submarine tragedy at Portland when H.M.S. *Sidon* was sunk as she lay alongside H.M.S. *Maidstone.* On 16 June 1955 fuel began leaking from a test torpedo in the sub's torpedo tubes. As pressure built up the fuel ignited and a tremendous explosion ripped through the *Sidon*, which began to go down. Despite heroic efforts by rescuers, one of whom lost his life in the attempt, three officers and ten ratings died in the sunken submarine. The photograph shows the *Sidon* being raised a week later.

Summer 1955 and extraordinary scenes in Weymouth and the surrounding villages. On the night of 18/19 July a record 11 inches of rain fell at Martinstown and the following day floods hit the villages of the River Wey. Here Upwey residents survey the flood damage in Church Street. There was tragedy at Broadwey when a twelve-year-old local lad drowned in a huge hole gouged out by flood waters.

Flooded Broadwey. This photograph was probably taken from the old Abbotsbury line railway bridge, looking along Watery Lane to Mill Street (the Mill can be seen top left). Houses have since been built on either side of the track (left) leading to the old station yard.

The Swannery car park looking across to Newstead Road and the buildings of the South Dorset Technical College.

Gloucester Street and Park Street residents paddle from their houses. In other areas of the town rowing boats rescued people stranded in their homes.

Westham Coach Park, looking towards Commercial Road. In the 1980s a new road system along the western shore of the Backwater completely altered the area shown in the foreground. In Gloucester Street the twin-spired Congregational Church has gone (now the site of George Thorne House) and the huge timber sheds in Commercial Road were demolished in the 1980s (now a car park).

Melcombe Regis Gardens' bowling green under water. The pavilion shown here was rebuilt in the 1990s.

A family of swans explore their expanded territory along Radipole Park Drive. Beyond the original bowling green pavilion can be seen Melcombe Regis School (later Weymouth Museum) and the Jubilee Hall, both now demolished.

Weymouth folk slipped and slithered to work in the big freeze of winter 1962/3 when the heaviest snowfalls for fifty years cut the town off from the rest of the county. The Arctic weather conditions brought tragedy when a Dorchester couple died in their car, buried in the snow on Osmington Hill. 70 passengers on two abandoned coaches had to be rescued after struggling through huge snowdrifts to reach the Clay Pigeon Café on the A37 and helicopters dropped food supplies to isolated villages in West Dorset. The temperature in Weymouth on 12 January 1963 was 19° F (13 degrees of frost). Here, frozen spray creates icy fringes along the Esplanade railings.

Piled snow at the top end of St Thomas Street.

The sea froze over!

A scene summer visitors to seaside Weymouth hope they won't experience! A gale-lashed and dramatic view of the Jubilee Clock in January 1965.

CHAPTER THREE

HARBOURSIDE

Ships of yesteryear and streets of old Weymouth

Spectators watching the *Premier* pass through the Town Bridge suggest an occasion of some kind and this was the paddle-steamer's last journey out of Weymouth on 29 April 1938. The veteran paddler, ninety-two years old and the oldest afloat had been in the port for eighty-six years. Sadly, her destination was the shipbreakers.

Cosens and Company's paddle-steamer *Victoria* passes through the Town Bridge, a welcome return after Second World War service. The company's fleet of pleasure steamers had been such a familiar feature of the harbour scene for more than a century that it was difficult to envisage holidays without a run to Lulworth or another of the coastal beauty spots. Sadly, their popularity waned and the last of the local paddlers left for the breakers' yard in 1967. It is ironic that today the last surviving paddle-steamer in the U.K., the *Waverley*, is packed with trippers every time she puts to sea.

Cosens' vessel *Emperor of India* steams across the Bay, on trials following a post-war rebuild in 1948. The paddle-steamer had joined the fleet as a two-year-old in 1908, having been rejected as unsuitable by the first company which owned her. Although Cosens also had problems with her (one of her captains said she was built more like a battleship than a paddle-steamer) the *Emperor of India* served the company for almost half a century. She was the only Cosens' vessel present at the evacuation of Dunkirk.

The *Emperor of India* leaving Weymouth for the shipbreakers in January 1957. There is no theatre in the background – it would be another year before rebuilding of the burnt-out Ritz began. The *St Julien* is just visible (left) and the lifeboat in the foreground is the long-serving *William and Clara Ryland.*

Captain Joseph Cosens introduced the first of his pleasure steamers to Weymouth in 1848. Countless thousands of locals and holidaymakers enjoyed sea trips for one hundred and twenty years before the last paddler *Embassy* left the port in 1967. *Consul* was acquired by Cosens in 1938, saw war service and then ran pleasure trips out of Weymouth until the 1960s. Fund-raising efforts to preserve her failed and *Consul* was seventy-two years old when she was finally despatched to the breakers in 1967. The photograph was taken in 1961.

Not in the Cosens' buff and black livery, for the *Princess Elizabeth* was operated by Coastal Steamers (Weymouth) during the summer seasons of 1963, 1964 and 1965. These were the last years of the steamer's active life – she was 'retired' in 1966 at the comparatively young age of thirty-nine having spent most of her working years with Red Funnel of Southampton. A traumatic period followed when it seemed she would become a rusting hulk until a businessman stepped in and refitted her as a floating club/restaurant moored just above London Bridge. She is now on the Continent.

The double, bow-fronted house in the centre of this photograph of Trinity Road was the summer home of Ralph Allen, wealthy and influential eighteenth-century Bath quarry owner. His regular visits in the 1750s and his enthusiasm for sea air and sea bathing helped to establish the town in its early days as a fashionable health and pleasure resort. Trinity Road and Nothe Parade form a picturesque and unspoilt backdrop to the harbour but just past Holy Trinity Church the pre-war scene of old shops and houses along North Quay and High Street changed dramatically following devastating air-raid damage.

All these buildings along North Quay and those in High Street behind them were demolished in the 1960s to make way for the present Municipal Offices and car parks. There was much protest and a Public Inquiry before No. 4 North Quay (far right) was pulled down in 1961 – it was a Tudor building of some note. Buildings beyond it had a brief stay of execution, but only until 1965, when they too were cleared. At Chapelhay, Holy Trinity School (top centre) had suffered Second World War bomb damage as had so much of this area, and it made way for post-war housing.

The building on the far left of the previous photograph was the Phoenix Stores (in the Fifties the premises of a fruit and veg. merchant) seen here shortly before its demolition in 1965.

Looking across the harbour in October 1965 just before the Phoenix building and neighbouring garage in the foreground were demolished. The brick-built office block 'Town Bridge House' adjacent to the old warehouses dates from 1958. Opposite, Pankhursts Motor Cycle showrooms occupied premises on the Town Bridge for many years in the former Palladium Cinema building (now a club).

This is the Tudor house, No. 4 North Quay, the proposed demolition of which caused such a furore in the 1950s. Its dilapidated condition belies its robust construction. From the early 1950s when plans were under discussion regarding the future development of the bomb-damaged streets along the harbourside, strenuous efforts were made to keep the historic old building. Individuals and local groups (particularly Weymouth Civic Society) campaigned for its conservation. All in vain. The decision of the Minister of Housing and Local Government following the Inspector's report of the proceedings of the public inquiry held in 1959 was that no preservation order should be made.

The Inspector's opinion was that if the building was retained:-

- it would not be possible to obtain the satisfactory layout for the planned Municipal Offices.
- the necessary road improvements could not be carried out.
- necessary restoration would lose some of the building's merit as an original example of the Tudor period.
- while at one time the Tudor House had formed an integral part of the harbour frontage, it would now stand by itself, a lone survivor.

The house in its harbour-side setting. No. 4 North Quay was demolished in August 1961.

A view of the North Quay site prior to clearance in 1961. The reconstruction of Chapelhay had begun during the previous decade and the new flats 'Chapelhay Heights' overlook the scene.

Neptune soft drinks were not manufactured at North Quay – this was the garage where the firm's delivery vehicles were kept. Occupants pre-war had included the charabancs of the local Greyhound company.

North Quay, partially demolished in 1961.

North Quay and the Municipal Offices of 1971. The building was officially opened on 1 June 1971 by H.R.H. Princess Anne in celebration of the borough's Quatercentenary. It was four hundred years since the two formerly quite separate towns of Weymouth, on the south side of the harbour and Melcombe Regis on the north had united as 'The Borough of Weymouth and Melcombe Regis' in 1571. Since local government reorganisation in 1974 its title has been 'The Borough of Weymouth and Portland'.

High Street was the heart of 'old' Weymouth before the Second World War bombs fell. It was, it seems, not much photographed before the war; a long winding every-day street not suited to the views on seaside postcards. It is remembered by many as a place of character and individuality. The remaining houses and businesses which once flourished here behind North Quay were also cleared in 1961. A few, such as the Fisherman's Arms, had gone a little earlier, probably due to their derelict and dangerous condition. Looking along old High Street from Boot Hill, the seventeenth-century Boot Inn, the Old Town Hall and the building behind it remain today. Demolition contractors are already at work further down the street.

Buildings beyond The Boot would soon be gone.

A little further down the street.

'Danger. Demolition. Keep Out.' The shop on the left was Harold Sanders 'Nutshell' of second-hand goods.

The building sprouting the inevitable 'bomb-site' buddleia bush was Oliver the fish merchant. Beyond was the 'Weymouth Arms' pub.

The end of High Street. The Phoenix building and adjacent garage survived until 1965.

A view looking towards Boot Hill. On the right is the rear of No. 4 North Quay. All the buildings in sight were razed – apart from the Old Town Hall, just visible in the left background.

The sadly dilapidated state of some of the High Street buildings before clearance. A number of them had been considered worthy of listing in the Inventory of the Royal Commission on Historical Monuments.

Pressure was mounting in the late-1950s for a speedier rebuilding of bomb-scarred Chapelhay, the area of the town which had suffered so much damage in the Second World War air raids. Prospect Place is seen here in 1957. The whole row was due to be demolished. The pub on the right of the picture was the Rising Sun.

None of these buildings exist today. The backs of the Prospect Row houses from the previous photograph are on the left. Chapelhay's post-war Prospect Inn was built here. On the right is the bombed Chapelhay Co-op in St Leonards Road. Franchise Street is in the foreground.

The front of the Co-op's shop in St Leonards Road. In the background the new shops of a re-sited 'Gordon Row' are in the course of construction.

The bombed butcher's shop of Mr Bartlett in Franchise Street in 1957, looking towards Boot Hill.

Chapelhay steps. All these buildings were demolished and the area they overlook at the rear of the Municipal Offices has since been landscaped.

Until late in the 1950s this massive early-nineteenth-century warehouse at the rear of the Guildhall dominated the harbour scene. Known as the 'Red Warehouse' it became increasingly dilapidated and was eventually demolished. For years the ugly space it left at the end of Lower St Mary Street was used as a car park but the site is now occupied by an extension to the Ship Inn on Custom House Quay.

April 1967 – North Quay has been cleared but work on the Municipal Offices has yet to begin.

14 June 1958 brought crowds to the harbourside for the official naming and dedication ceremony of a new lifeboat – the *Frank Spiller Locke* paid for from the generous legacy of Dr Locke, of Tunbridge Wells, to the R.N.L.I. This was a 52-foot Barnett-type boat, the largest in production at the time. The *Frank Spiller Locke* was in service at Weymouth until 1976.

A 1954 view of Weymouth Harbour from Trinity Terrace. The two large vessels at the pier are the cross-channel ferries *St Helier/St Julien* and the *St Patrick.* Close by (between the cranes) can be seen the sagging girders of the burnt-out Ritz Theatre, destroyed by fire in April of that year. Still very much in use was the Weymouth Harbour Tramway, as indicated by the long line of railway wagons on the Quay. The Tramway operated between 1865 and 1988 taking trains from Weymouth Station along the familiar railway lines which run through the streets to the Quay.

Both G.W.R. vessels in this 1957 photograph served with distinction at Dunkirk. The *Roebuck* (foreground) took 600 men, including wounded, back to Dover. Both *Roebuck* and her sister ship *Sambur* went on Admiralty service for the rest of the war. The *St Helier's* record at Dunkirk was outstanding. In eight crossings she brought more than 10 000 troops and 1500 refugees to safety. Her captain and two of his officers were awarded the D.S.C. and the quartermaster received the D.S.M.

A reminder of the days when Weymouth handled cargo on a regular basis. Adam Lythgoe lorries stretch as far as the eye can see awaiting the unloading of the Dutch vessel *Rian's* cargo of basic slag at the newly-constructed cargo stage in 1954. In the background, resembling a giant game of 'cat's cradle' are the twisted girders of the burnt-out Ritz Theatre.

The G.W.R.'s *Roebuck* at the cargo stage in September 1957. By this time the remains of the Ritz Theatre had been removed but work was not to start on building the present 'Pavilion' until the autumn of the following year.

Prior to the arrival of the *Caesarea* and *Sarnia* in 1961, the *St Patrick* was the pride of the Weymouth fleet. She was the last ship ever built for the G.W.R., launched in 1947. Her own flags and the flag decked vessel in the background suggest that this is her arrival day at Weymouth in 1948.

New vessels on the Weymouth/Channel Islands route in 1961 were the *Caesarea* and *Sarnia* (from the Roman names for Jersey and Guernsey). They were to be the last of the traditional Channel Island passenger ferries. From 1973 car ferries were introduced and when the *Sarnia* left Weymouth in 1977 the service was operated solely by car ferries. In the 1980s hydrofoils took over and the harbour scene today is dominated by these giant craft.

A good selection of the port's cargo and passenger vessels in the harbour, October 1961. In the cove is the *Roebuck* – her sister ship *Sambur* is on the opposite side of the harbour. The two vessels had arrived in Weymouth in 1925 and were nearing the end of their time here, both going for scrap in the mid-1960s. The three passenger ferries visible are the *St Patrick*, *Caesarea* and *Sarnia*.

A view which has become almost a classic over the years – 'Weymouth Harbour from the Nothe'. On this occasion the ship framed by the trees is the *Caesarea*, leaving for the Channel Islands in April 1961.

In post-Second World War years the Royal Navy at Portland played an important role in sea training. Battleships and aircraft carriers served in the Portland Training Squadron. The aircraft carrier *Indefatigable* was a familiar sight in the waters around Weymouth in the early-1950s.

Weymouth regularly hosts sailing events. This crowded beach scene in 1959 is of the National 12's dinghy racing championships.

Two superb photographs of 12-metre yachts in Weymouth Bay in 1962.

Commercial Road, viewed from across the Backwater in the early-1960s. A very changed scene here today. All the waterfront buildings the length of Commercial Road were removed and only two recent structures – the Marina and the Angling Society H.Q. – stand on the west side of Commercial Road now. Along the 'town' side of the road the Jubilee Hall and buildings shown to the right of it have gone – replaced by Debenhams and the 'New Bond Street' development.

All the buildings shown in Commercial Road have been demolished (the lamp post shown on the left was at the end of Mulberry Terrace).

A scene at the bottom of Boot Hill, almost unrecognisable today. Behind the car/coach park in the foreground are the retort houses of Weymouth Gasworks. These came down in 1962 and Westwey House now stands on the site. The area along Westwey Road was once the heart of industrial Weymouth. The tall chimney of Sunneybank Power Station is in the centre of the photograph.

Enlargement of the Gasworks site on Westwey Road in the 1950s included the addition of a new gasholder, the foundations of which were installed in 1955. The large retort house on the right of the previous photograph was part of this extension. The paddle-steamer in the centre of the picture is the *Emperor of India.* Both waterfront and skyline on the Melcombe shore are vastly changed today.

An unusual 'aerial' shot of Weymouth Backwater taken from the older gasholder at Weymouth Gasworks (its steel framework is visible on the next photograph). Of the three church spires in the centre of the 1950s picture only the most northerly – St John's – remains today. Christchurch (centre) was demolished in 1956/7 and the twin spires of Gloucester Street Congregational Church came down in 1971. Both sites were redeveloped.

Sunneybank Electricity Generating Station, Westwey Road in 1960. Power supply commenced from here on 26 September 1904 and Sunneybank was owned and operated by Weymouth Corporation from 1904 until nationalisation in 1947. Rendered obsolete by advances in technology and power distribution, it was demolished in 1974. Much of Westwey Road has been re-developed in recent years. The St John Ambulance HQ of 1939 (on the right of the picture) was found to be structurally unsafe and was completely rebuilt in 1994.

Westham Bridge in the early-1960s. The bridge closed to traffic in 1987 when a new road scheme incorporating the newly constructed 'Swannery Bridge' across the Backwater came into use. At the time this photograph was taken Melcombe Regis School (centre) was still in use. It closed in 1970 and a year later re-opened as the town's first Museum. When the Museum relocated to Brewer's Quay in 1989 the 1912 school building was knocked down and Weymouth Marina now stands on this site.

Looking towards Westham. The building in the centre of the picture is the Health Centre of 1930.

Straddling the Backwater and resembling a giant Meccano set, this is the Westham end of the steel viaduct which carried the Weymouth and Portland railway line across the lake from Melcombe Regis station. It replaced an earlier timber bridge in 1909 and lasted until 1974 when work on its removal began. Here, a gas main is being secured to the viaduct in 1958. The lines of the old miniature railway run along the shore beneath it.

Weymouth's new bus garage in the mid-1950s. Its predecessor on the same site in Edward Street had been destroyed during an air raid in October 1940. The western shore of the Backwater/Radipole Lake was completely changed by the construction of a relief road (Weymouth Way) in the 1980s. A road bridge has since replaced the railway viaduct, the line to Portland having closed to passengers in 1952 and goods in 1965. The previous picture was taken from the 'far shore' and the 'terminus' of the miniature railway can be seen on the far left of this photograph.

Noah's Ark Aquarium came to 'berth' on Radipole Lake in 1966. It was an attraction there for several years before it transferred to premises on Weymouth seafront and eventually closed. The 'Ark', never a floating structure but built on a concrete platform, became an Amusement Arcade before its conversion to a restaurant.

The second photograph of Noah's Ark shows a clear view up the lake following the removal of the iron viaduct in the 1970s. It was not to last – a road bridge, part of the 1980s relief road scheme, now spans the lake once again.

A stroll along the attractive Rose Walk in Melcombe Regis Gardens led to the Corporation greenhouses. The railway viaduct can be seen on the left, crossing Radipole Park Drive.

Radipole Lake viewed from Westham Coach Park in 1956. Passengers alighting here made their way across Westham Bridge en route to and from the beach and brought good trade to the shopkeepers in Westham Road. The coach parking area is long gone and the whole shore here was redeveloped in the 1980s when the relief road was constructed. This group has arrived by coach from Bristol on a works outing and smiling faces suggest that a day trip to the seaside in the Fifties was a real treat.

Not quite 'the end of the pier show', but an attractive view of the tower structure at the end of the stone pier, 1961. Then, as now, a popular spot for fishing.

CHAPTER FOUR

GOING TO TOWN

Shopping, with a few diversions along the way

Dating from around 1970 is this rather alarming photograph of traffic congestion at the St Thomas Street/Westham Road junction. On the plus side St Thomas Street is free of parked cars and a one-way traffic system appears to operate as far as Forte's Corner.

'Forte's Corner' – so long a local place name that it is still in use, although Forte's Ice Cream Parlor has been replaced by the Hogshead pub. Rocco Forte opened several restaurants and cafés along the south coast in the 1920s. These were the foundations of Trust House Forte which later became the world's biggest hotel and catering business. His son Charles (later Sir Charles) Forte managed the Weymouth restaurants as a young man.

W.H. Smith the bookseller had occupied this building for just over fifty years when the photograph was taken in 1956. In the 1990s the business moved down the street to much larger premises.

Now a restaurant and baker, Nos 6-7 Coburg Place were formerly occupied by a rather exclusive ladies-wear shop. Dwarfed by its tall neighbour the little early-nineteenth-century building adds old-fashioned charm amidst a sea of plate glass. The very large oval plaque on its wall announced in 1977 that this was also the office of the Danish vice-consulate.

This handsome building replaced Victorian 'Royal Baths' on the site in the late-1920s. It originally comprised an assortment of small shops (including Edwin Jones) with a restaurant above. Linking St Thomas Street and St Mary Street was the Clinton Arcade, much appreciated by shoppers and holidaymakers as a short cut between the main streets and a shelter in the wet weather. Edwin Jones eventually took over the whole building. Date of this photograph is 1961.

An earlier picture of the bustling arcade with its individual shops. The ladies are wearing the 'swagger' coats typical of the mid-Fifties.

Summer fashions 1959 – an Edwin Jones window display.

Because the Clinton Arcade allowed free access between the streets it was often assumed to be a public right of way. It was not, and the owners were careful not to let it become one through common usage. Every year, on Good Friday, gates were erected to bar entry to the arcade. Judging from this desolate scene the weather for this Easter Bank Holiday weekend in the 1950s was not too promising!

When Edwin Jones expanded, the arcade disappeared although everyone used the shop as a short cut much as they had done before. Today separate businesses occupy the building and there is no way through.

The photographic business founded by Graham Herbert's father was at 9 Coburg Place, at the top end of St Thomas Street.

This building, once the H.Q. of Weymouth Waterworks Company, was a furniture store for many years. The Jays chain occupied it in 1957 when this photograph was taken. It and other premises in Lower Bond Street were to remain empty and boarded up in the early-1990s as various town centre development schemes were heralded but fell through. In the late-1990s the planned shopping centre was finally achieved and the street renamed 'New Bond Street'. The store shown here was completely rebuilt but the developers continued the tradition of a tower feature on the new building.

Apart from the National Provincial Bank (NatWest today) and the White Hart pub (left) all these buildings in Lower Bond Street have gone. If the shoppers crossing the street glanced left today Debenhams department store would face them, and new shops line the renamed 'New Bond Street'.

Looking up St Thomas Street (Jays' successor was Woodhouse Furniture) the old cinema entrance is just visible.

The cinema was a conversion of the Victorian Jubilee Hall set way back from the street. The Hall was demolished in 1989 in readiness for a new shopping centre and at the same time these single-storey structures were removed, revealing the red brick 'Old Rectory' behind. Built in the early-nineteenth century it has been meticulously restored and is now owned by the Hobgoblins wine bar chain.

Entrance into the cinema was via a long corridor from the street…

… into the splendid 1920s auditorium. The cinema adopted the name 'Regent' in 1926 later becoming the Gaumont, Odeon and New Invicta before cinema audiences gave way to bingo players. It closed in 1977. These pictures date from 1968.

More views of Lower Bond Street. At Nos 9-11 the Lamb and Flag public house closed in the late-1950s. The little lane beside the pub was Harmony Court.

In 1961 the pub was converted to a branch of Aggie Weston's, the sailor's 'home from home', which in turn closed in 1974.

At the far end of Lower Bond Street Kennedys builders' merchants opened new showrooms in 1955. These stood on the historic site of the Queen's Barracks, cavalry barracks dating back to the days of King George III's visits to the town. In the twentieth century the barracks became known as Burdon's Buildings, a very overcrowded slum tenement which was pulled down in the 1920s. The Regent Garage was here prior to Kennedys.

Weymouth's first large supermarket was the International Superstore of 1978, in Lower Bond Street with adjacent multi-storey car park. To provide the site, a little town centre street – Bury Street, a row of cottages, a chapel and burial ground – disappeared altogether in the mid-1970s. Now the supermarket, too, is no more and the Multiplex cinema of the New Bond Street development stands here.

A return to St Thomas Street, and so much has changed here since 1956! No. 73, Hallett the furnisher is now No. 74, estate agent Roger McGhee. Next door the Southern Gas Board has become Abbey National's building society premises. The Southern Gas Showrooms were completely demolished and the modern replacement block houses two shops – Joseph Weld's charity shop and Blockbuster video. Porter the fruiterer is Homes and Gardens. The next very ornate building still stands, its ground floor much altered and housing Clark's shoe shop. Photographs of Thurman's and Groves, either side of the Post Office, follow.

Thurman's, long-established ironmonger in St Thomas Street. The shop occupied what had originally been an eighteenth-century three-storey town house. When Thurman's closed in the 1960s and a supermarket took over it was stipulated that although alterations could be carried out, the façade above ground floor level must be restored. The Iceland chain currently occupies No. 68.

A complete change of scene here on the corner of St Thomas Street and Lower St Alban Street. This imposing building was the registered office of Groves the brewers. The merger of Groves and Devenish in 1960 left the offices redundant. In 1966 they were completely demolished and a familiar supermarket chain –Tesco – erected the present store on the site.

The *Dorset Echo* office in St Thomas Street was rebuilt following severe damage during one of Weymouth's worst air raids on 2 April 1942. For the early period of the photographs in this book the newspaper was the *Dorset Daily Echo*, retitled *Dorset Evening Echo* in 1958. Now it is the *Dorset Echo* and in 1999 moved to large premises on the Granby Industrial Estate west of the town. This building, seen here in 1962, has since been converted to a wine lodge.

Tilleys Motor Showrooms were three doors along from the *Echo* office at No. 60 St Thomas Street. The Wessex Trustee Savings Bank moved here next and now the Toad wine bar chain occupies these premises.

Three long-established businesses in the town centre, in one picture. On the left, V.H. Bennett's department store, later taken over by Debenhams. Centre, the electrical goods dealer Bennett and Escott. Then the Jersey Tavern which closed in 1999 and has recently re-opened as a coffee shop.

Traffic chaos in St Thomas Street in 1964. The pedestrianisation of Weymouth's two main shopping streets was then more than twenty years in the future. Buildings in the right foreground were demolished in 1975. When Weatherspoons took over the replacement buildings in the 1990s the company adopted the old 'Swan Inn' name for the new pub on the site.

St Edmund Street. Ward's shop originally extended to the corner of the building, but Platts grocery store had taken over in the 1950s. (Now Dodgsons D.I.Y.).

Self-service shops were introduced in the Fifties and Platts was the first in Weymouth. Some long-established brand names are on display here!

In St Edmund Street the Golden Lion Hotel was originally a coaching inn of the eighteenth century or earlier. Its past landlords no doubt had a fund of interesting stories to tell but the 'Tail' of the Golden Lion is one of the twentieth century. Dates assigned to the incident vary, but the Golden Lion's original curly tail disappeared back to camp with a group of merry U.S. servicemen in the run-up to D-Day 1944. The landlord effected a temporary repair using a pick-axe handle, suitably gilded, and the lion stood guarding the entrance door with his rigid tail held aloft for many years until brewers Devenish restored his pride and his curly tail. The lion is seen here with his pick-axe tail (some say it was a broom handle) in 1954.

A fragment of the old town put to a very modern use. This Stuart building at the junction of St Edmund Street and Maiden Street bears the scar of seventeenth-century battle. A cannon ball fired during English Civil War fighting is embedded high in the wall. Before public conveniences were installed on the ground floor, the building housed the town's fire engine. The Guildhall along the street dates from 1837, the first year of Queen Victoria's reign.

V.H. Bennett's department store occupied the whole of the St Thomas Street/Bond Street/St Mary Street corner. It was taken over by Debenhams, who left the town in 1982 but returned in 1999 to operate from a large new store in the New Bond Street development.

Shoppers a-plenty at the first day of Bennett's Summer Sale in July 1959.

When Debenhams vacated the store a huge rebuilding programme was necessary to reinforce and modernise the premises which had been added to piecemeal over the years as Mr Bennett increased the size of his shop. Beneath the plastic shrouds in the 1980s work in progress included the superb restoration of the façade above the ground floor. This is now W.H. Smith.

Two rather desolate scenes from 1961 – a boarded-up town centre shop and road surfaces which appear to be in need of some attention. Sargeant was a jeweller and pawnbroker whose premises extended from St Mary Street back to New Street via Blockhouse Lane. The business had closed and the stock in trade was up for sale. The whole of Sargeants premises was rebuilt. As, later, was Woolworths beyond, a large art-deco tiled building of great style.

New Street and the end of Blockhouse Lane – all now redeveloped.

Edwin Jones 'Bon Marche' department store at the lower end of St Mary Street in 1964. Courts Furnishers moved into this shop in 1969, later extending through to St Thomas Street when the firm took over the former Hawkes, Freeman store.

Until 1939 the Victorian Market House stood here – a large and impressive 1855 building containing shops and stalls. The popularity of indoor markets seemed to be on the wane in the Thirties and as no other use was found for the building it was demolished. Only the end wall abutting on to St Mary's Churchyard remained, and it can be seen here, part of the present 'Market House'. A central arcade links St Mary Street and Maiden Street. Refurbishment in the 1990s modernised this rather dull façade.

A quartet of Weymouth shopfronts. Gifts for everyone in the jam-packed Christmas display at Hawkes, Freeman in 1961. The firm, established in Weymouth since 1845, had been taken over by Webb, Major and Co. Ltd in 1955 but kept its original name. These premises in St Thomas Street are currently occupied by Courts Furnishers.

Sweet shops are almost a thing of the past now, with every kind of shop selling pre-packaged chocolates and confectionery. Roberts had shops in both main streets – this one in St Mary Street had curved windows which were slightly odd to look into. Roberts manufactured their own boiled sweets in Weymouth and they were sold throughout the county.

Defying changing fashions in signwriting and today very much back in fashion is Moores art-deco shop sign in Westham Road. It dates from the 1930s when the shop (selling then, as now, handbags and jewellery) was built.

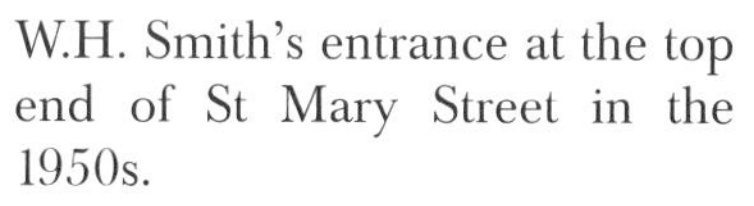
W.H. Smith's entrance at the top end of St Mary Street in the 1950s.

Steward's Court, Devenish Square and part of Governor's Lane were demolished soon after these photographs were taken late in the 1950s. This is Governor's Lane looking towards East Street. The buildings on the right remain. All on the left have gone – this is now East Street Car Park.

An old stone doorway may have been a fragment of the town's medieval Friary. Beyond it the very end of the 'Steward's Court' street sign is just visible.

Steward's Court, the little alley of houses off Governor's Lane. The street sign is the same as in the previous picture. There were some 12 houses in the Court and they are remembered with affection by those who lived there.

A fragment of Weymouth's theatrical history in St Nicholas Street. This arch led theatre-goers in Victorian times to the 'Theatre Royal' in a converted chapel at the back of this site. The theatre closed before the end of the nineteenth century, was converted to a store and pulled down in the 1960s. The entrance arch lasted until the 1980s, when it, too, was removed. The town had an earlier Theatre Royal on the Esplanade in the days of King George III's visits.

Weymouth Harbour Tramway, horse-drawn when it first began operating in the 1860s, took trains from Weymouth Station through the streets to the harbour. It went out of use in 1988 with the introduction of electric trains to Weymouth, but the lines remain. G.W.R. pannier tank engines were in use when this photograph was taken in 1958. This is No. 1367, the first of these engines to be permanently allocated to the service. It arrived in 1935 and stayed until 1962. Note the official with the warning red flag who preceded it through the streets! The train is about to pass the end of Westham Road.

Almost the same spot, in 1965. By this date diesels had completely taken over on the Tramway. Progress through the town was slow – the trains travelled at 5 m.p.h. and carelessly parked cars on occasion brought the journey to a complete halt.

Pubs are re-named today with such regularity it is difficult to keep pace with the changes. Devenish's Prince Albert Inn on the corner of Westham Road and Great George Street dates from the late-1930s,built in the then fashionable mock-Tudor style. It became O'Flannigan's and is currently Finn McCouls. Just along Great George Street was the tall building of Hallett's furniture repository. It and adjacent houses have since been replaced by apartments.

The 'Co-op' first arrived in Weymouth in the 1860s and the firm's big department store in Westham Road opened in 1926. It closed in 1999 although other Co-op stores still flourish in and around the town. Wilkinsons now occupy the Westham Road store.

Christchurch in King Street and a glimpse of the old railway station in 1956. Vaux the Baker's van (bottom corner) was well known in the town – it was shaped like a bread loaf.

The church, an impressive building of some size, had a comparatively short life. It was consecrated in 1874 but declared redundant in the 1930s. The decision to demolish Christchurch came in the 1950s and shops and flats (Garnet Court) now stand on the site. This is the view along Park Street.

Christchurch, scaffolded and ready for demolition in 1956.

Commemorative items left in the church spire in 1874. Sadly they had deteriorated over eighty years – a local newspaper and a large poster announcing that 'the walls of this church being now nearly complete' a special inauguration service would be held at the parish church, St Mary's.

Graham Herbert's photograph of Park Street, taken from the tower of Christchurch. Gloucester Street Congregational Church and the huge timber sheds would disappear within the next thirty years.

Again, from the tower. Ranelagh Road is in the foreground, with Eldridge Pope's Ranelagh Hotel on the corner still in business in 1956. Queen Street (the Clifton Hotel and Digby's Arcade are on the right) runs up to Tilley's corner and Victoria Street.

Stunning views of Weymouth railway station taken from the tower of Christchurch shortly before the church's demolition in 1956. Christchurch stood opposite the station, at the junction of King Street and Park Street.

A major expansion to Weymouth station was planned in the 1930s but was abandoned when war broke out. Partial modernisation in the 1950s did not include new station buildings and Brunel's somewhat altered original G.W.R. design was one hundred and thirty years old and in a rather dilapidated state when it was finally replaced in 1986. Much of the railway land on the left-hand side of the pictures is now occupied by shops and businesses.

A new signal box for Weymouth in 1956 – the foundations of which can be seen here, at the end of Ranelagh Road. It came into operation in April the following year.

The era of steam ended at Weymouth on 8 July 1967 when Merchant Navy Class Loco No. 35023 Blue Funnel Line brought the last steam-hauled passenger train on the Waterloo/Weymouth line into Weymouth Station. Seen here at Weymouth is No. 35013, an engine of the same class.

Tilley's Garage and Motor Showrooms, 1957. The garage occupied a large site on the corner of Victoria Street until the 1970s, in later years owned by Wadham Stringer. An apartment block, Nightingale Court, replaced it.

CHAPTER FIVE

ON THE PROM

Holiday scenes of yesterday and reminders of an elegant age

Could there possibly have been room for one more family on the beach? Weymouth in the late-1950s. Cheap foreign travel and package holidays abroad were a few years in the future and the English seaside was still the popular choice.

A nice detail of the wooden façade of the Ritz Theatre before fire destroyed it in 1954. Sited in front of the entrance was the Clark and Endicott Memorial, its plaque commemorating sixteenth- and seventeenth-century voyagers out of Weymouth. The memorial was moved to a spot in the Alexandra Gardens when the present Pavilion Theatre was under construction, but it is deserving of a more prominent location.

The location of the Arcade in Crescent Street. Both this and the previous view are 1950s photographs.

Parking problems and traffic jams were a constant theme in the 1950s. This was the car park in Gloucester Mews in 1959. The garage (left) was Channons. Gloucester Street Congregational Church was pulled down (its foundations were insubstantial) in 1971, providing the site for 'George Thorne House'.

Snapped! This is photographer Graham Herbert on top of a portable tower and filming the new Pavilion Theatre in 1960.

Exterior and interior views of the new Pavilion. The theatre opened on 14 July 1960, with 'Let's Make a Night of It' starring Benny Hill.

Made largely from Chesil Beach pebbles and shells, the decorative mermaid panels on the front of the building eventually succumbed to the vagaries of English seaside weather. Having become rather dilapidated, they were covered over in the 1980s.

The Alexandra Gardens Theatre closed in 1963; competition with the newer Pavilion proved too great. The theatre in the Gardens had replaced the 'Kursaal' – a building constructed largely of glass, in 1924.

Hollands Amusements took over the theatre and much of the gardens in 1964. In September 1993 the former theatre burned down and a new amusements centre now fills the site.

The 'Clarence Hotel' name is no more. The premises have been extended to include the neighbouring insurance office and this is now the 'Rex Hotel' behind the Alexandra Gardens.

This Georgian building at the southern end of the Esplanade is currently a night-club, an entertainment venue for holidaymakers and residents. Not, perhaps, such a great change of use since its eighteenth-century heyday as John Harvey's 'Library and Card Assembly', although the 'holidaymakers' then were the wealthy and privileged who could afford to spend weeks or even months 'taking the cure' at the seaside. Harvey's 'Rooms' were a place to chat and gossip, play cards, read the latest newspapers and books or take part in a sedate formal dance. The 'lower orders' enjoyed rather more boisterous evenings in the local taverns. For many years this was HQ for the Royal Dorset Yacht Club.

No. 6 Chesterfield Place disappeared in 1964 when the Marks and Spencer store was extended. Then, 'The Esplanade' consisted of a series of individually named and numbered terraces but in the early-1970s buildings along the length of 'the prom' were numbered consecutively as The Esplanade. The street signs bearing the former terrace names can still be seen, a reminder of the town's Georgian heritage. In 1964, No. 6 Chesterfield Place (itself a replacement of an earlier building on the site) had already lost its original street frontage to modern plate glass.

The upper floors are taken down.

The completed extension, indistinguishable from the adjacent 1930s Marks and Spencer building.

Statue House in the 1960s looking very much as it does today. In 1953 plans were afoot to radically alter this listed building by inserting modern shop fronts at pavement level – a scheme firmly rejected by the Ministry of Housing and Local Government.

Heated discussions centred on the King's Statue in the 1950s. One of the proposals of a scheme designed to ease Weymouth's traffic congestion was that the Statue should be moved (at considerable cost) to another site on the Esplanade 'Why keep it at all?' asked some. 'Dump it in the sea,' suggested others. Eventually the council abandoned the plan to move the monument. King George III stayed where he was and a large traffic roundabout was laid out around the Statue (which is now a Grade I listed building).

Some refurbishment of the Portland stone plinth was carried out at the same time. The Statue itself, made of Coade stone, was painted in heraldic colours for the first time in 1949, one hundred and forty years after the foundation stone was laid.

The Gloucester Hotel still stands, converted now to offices and apartments. Important in Weymouth's seaside history, it was the summer home of King George III, built by his brother William Henry, Duke of Gloucester. The King spent 14 holidays here between 1789 and 1805, the first to recuperate from the 'madness' which had so alarmed the nation. By royal standards it was a modest home and not large enough to accommodate the vast entourage which accompanied the Royal family. Many servants were 'boarded-out', rising early to scurry across town and carry out their duties at 'Royal Lodge'. The horizontal band of white stone running across the façade denotes the height of the original house. An extra storey was added following a severe fire in 1927. The large Victorian block adjoining at the southern end dates from the Gloucester's conversion to an hotel in the mid-nineteenth century. A succession of verandahs has partially obscured the ground floor, but it is quite possible that King George may have stood at one of the Venetian arched windows (right) gazing at the chilly waters of Weymouth Bay and wondering if he would enjoy bathing in the sea (he did, and his return visits brought the town fame as 'Royal Weymouth').

This sunny terrace was removed when the basement of the building opened up as a pub.

A third view from the 1950s, looking out across the Bay. Framed in the Gloucester's doorway is a G.W.R. steamer – the *St Helier* or *St Julien*, leaving port on the regular crossing to the Channel Islands.

An elegant bow-fronted Georgian building of the same name is long gone, replaced by this second 'Royal Hotel' of the 1890s. It has all the extravagant heavy detailing of the late-Victorian period and makes a striking centrepiece in the midst of the more austere style of its Georgian neighbours.

The ground-floor balcony panels feature the ship from the town's coat-of-arms.

Commemorative monument, focal point, meeting place and controversial site of the 1988 subway construction, the Jubilee Clock is Weymouth's best-known landmark. In May 1961 40 revered and elderly motor cars chugged along the Esplanade for the first Veteran Car Club Rally to be held in the resort. Some of the vehicles were almost as old as the Clock – erected in 1887 to celebrate the Golden Jubilee of Queen Victoria.

Weymouth's War Memorial, an 18ft high column of Portland stone stands on the Esplanade opposite the Prince Regent Hotel. The ceremony pictured here took place in February 1963 during the South West area conference of the British Legion. This was the severe winter of 1962/3 and very few of the expected delegates reached Weymouth due to snow, ice and foggy conditions on the roads.

The present 'Prince Regent Hotel' was formerly the Hotel Burdon. Dating from the 1850s it is a great contrast to the ornate 'Royal' of the later Victorian period. The Burdon and its neighbours echo the simpler lines of the Georgian seafront terraces. The Burdon, up for sale in the 1950s, was considered as a new home for Weymouth's Municipal Offices (then in Clarence Buildings). The possible loss of one of Weymouth's biggest hotels was much decried and the owner eventually decided to stay in business. It was 1971 before the Municipal Offices moved to new purpose-built premises on North Quay.

Local opinion regarding the Pier Bandstand varied greatly. When it first opened in 1939 many felt its short pier feature spoilt the long continuous sweep of Weymouth Bay and the rather lopsided piles which supported it gave the structure a rather tumbledown appearance. The bandstand buildings, though, were an art deco delight. Many recall fond memories of summer evening dances held on its open air deck, occasionally interrupted by rain and a dash for the shelters along its sides. The 'pier' of the Pier Bandstand was blown up in 1986 but the building on the Esplanade remains, refurbished in the late-1990s.

The Pier Bandstand sun deck, a pleasant sheltered spot with uninterrupted sea views.

Some of the entertainments on offer at the Pier Bandstand in the 1960s.

CHAPTER 6

HOLIDAY HIGHLIGHTS

Sun, sand, sea and stars

Dancing the night away… 30 July 1958 was a record night at the Pier Bandstand when Ted Heath and his Music played to 1600 dancers at the late-night Jazz Ball.

Wrestling at the neon-lit Pier Bandstand in 1958. Well-known names billed to appear included Jackie Pallo, Tibor Szakacs and Johnny Czeslaw.

The Pier Bandstand hosted many regular events over the years – open-air dancing, band concerts, roller skating and wrestling among them – and it was also the venue for beauty contests. In the summertime, weekly heats in the competition to become 'Miss Weymouth' were a popular attraction.

This was the line-up for the final in August 1959. The winner was twenty-year-old Judith Edwards from Redditch, Worcestershire (second from top).

Fashionable 'beehive' hairdos were much in evidence at the final of the 1963 'Miss Weymouth' competition. The winner, Jackie Peterson of Brighton, was a hairdresser and she sported the least lacquered hairstyle in the line-up! Runners-up were local girls Daphne Dagger (far right) and Suzanne McQuiston (far left) who was the year's Carnival Queen.

Traditionally, the storylines are violent, the characters unpleasant and the voices raucous, but children delight in the knockabout comedy of the Punch and Judy show. Apart from the Pier Bandstand in the background there is little to distinguish this beach scene from one of today.

'Holiday Playtimes' on the sands, usually sponsored by a national newspaper or magazine publisher, were a jolly seaside mix of games, competitions and fancy dress. On the pier can be seen the temporary replacement of the burnt-down Ritz Theatre – a Big Top featuring an ice pantomime in August 1956. A smaller marquee used for dancing had unfortunately blown away in a severe gale the previous month!

Crew members of the U.S.S. *Nautilus* joined the 'Holiday Playtime' crowds in 1958 after the submarine's famous voyage under the Polar ice.

There is a long tradition of creating models made only of sand and sea water at Weymouth. Jack Hayward began displaying his work in the 1920s and was famous for his miniature cathedrals. This one dates from the 1950s. Vandalism is nothing new and Mr Hayward and his partner undertook all-night vigils beside the model at the height of the season to protect the fragile structure from damage.

Jack Hayward's successor was Fred Darrington who brought colour to the beach with lively scenes featuring sculpted and painted figures (apart from the paint, the only 'ingredients' were still only Weymouth sand and sea water). Fred's grandson Mark is now the resort's summer sand modeller.

A very unseasonal holiday highlight – Weymouth's golden sands were being loaded on to three lorries for transport to Olympia in January 1963. The excavator had taken time out from shovelling snow during the exceptionally cold winter. The sand (plus 120 gallons of Weymouth sea water) was destined for a Holiday Exhibition where a display of Fred Darrington's art was a feature of the resort's publicity drive.

The Alexandra Garden Theatre closed at the end of the 1963 season and Hollands Amusements took over. The thatched shelter was the last of the six put up around the perimeter of the gardens in the early-1900s and it too was later removed.

Donkey rides on the sands, a holiday feature at Weymouth since Victorian times, are no more. Len Downton, whose family had owned and run the donkeys for more than one hundred years, retired in 2000 and his donkeys retired with him. This 1950s carriage ride was a variation on the traditional amble along the beach.

Commemorative floral displays have been an annual feature at Greenhill Gardens for many years. Mayor Lucie Hill admires the 6000-plus plants which made up the 'National Savings Week' emblem in 1966.

Weymouth's traditional August Carnival was suspended during the war years but restarted in 1952. In 1955 the Carnival procession took a route across the Town Bridge. Wyke Regis Community Association's 'Swan Lake' tableau was a first prizewinner.

1958 and Portwey Hospital's float is ready to move off in Newstead Road. A few changes here – the Cornopean Inn, the shop on the opposite corner and Portwey Hospital have all closed. A.J. Digby, the firm of fruit and vegetable merchants which supplied the lorry no longer exists.

Rain dampened the 1956 procession. Carnival Queen Jennifer Hinde of Wyke Regis is in the leading float with her attendants Pearl Spiller and Pat Wardingham.

Admiralty Underwater Weapons Establishment staff won the Round Table Cup for 'St George and the Dragon'.

Highlight in Weymouth's 1958 carnival was the appearance of the 751st United States Third Air Force Band leading the procession. At the U.S. D-Day Memorial on the Esplanade two plaques commemorating the occasion were presented to the band.

Portland Navy Days offered the chance to look over H.M. ships and meet the men of the Royal Navy. Open to view in August 1958 were the cruiser H.M.S. *Birmingham*, frigates H.M.S. *Pellew*, *Malcolm* and *Dundas* and submarines H.M.S. *Sea Scout* and *Solent*. The queues indicate how popular this three-day event was – 20 000-plus visitors paid a very reasonable 1s./6d. for five and a half hours' entertainment which included naval aircraft displays, music by the band of the Royal Marines and free boat trips round the harbour.

'Hello, my darlin's', as a bedraggled Charlie Drake paddles ashore. Charlie was starring in the 1958 Alexandra Gardens summer show. The dressing gown, bath and four hours of outdoor filming by a B.B.C. camera crew were for a slot on the T.V. programme '6.5 Special' featuring his comedy record 'Splish Splash'.

Star of the first summer show at the new Pavilion Theatre when it opened in July 1960 was Benny Hill in 'Let's Make a Night of It' with Cyril Stapleton and his Show Band. At the Alexandra Gardens Theatre the same month top of the bill was singer Anne Shelton, with Morecombe and Wise also appearing. Benny Hill is seen here with the chorus of Weymouth Operatic Society.

The Dick Emery Show was the summer attraction at the Pavilion Theatre in 1965 and the star was out and about filming character roles for his TV series. In St Alban Street he is Hettie the spinster, ready to pounce on her hapless interviewer with the inevitable 'Are you married? I'm looking for a nice young man…'

On Custom House Quay he plays the blue-blazered yachting type to a crowd of amused spectators.

The 1970 summer season brought Tommy Trinder to the Pavilion, posing here with the show's dancers.

The miniature express 4-4-2 'Merrie England' nears the end of the line at Westham in 1958. The line, the fairground and the girder bridge across Radipole Lake are no more. Weymouth Way now runs along the lake's western shore.

Chipperfields Fun Fair occupied this site on the western shore of Radipole Lake. The brick arch on the right carried the railway line of the Weymouth and Portland Railway but is best remembered as the entrance to the coach park and fun fair (now the site of a traffic roundabout, part of the 1980s road scheme). A great many of the buildings in the background of this photograph have also since been demolished.

One of the fair's best-remembered rides was the 'Wild Mouse' which threatened to tip its carriages' occupants into the lake at every sharp turn.

The circus was in town in July and August 1964 and Chipperfields laid on various publicity stunts to advertise their shows at Lodmoor. Elephants were bathed in the sea, tiger cubs posed with pretty girls and clowns in full make-up clowned around. Most bizarre was the visit of a circus camel to the Old Coopers Arms pub (now Brunches restaurant) in Maiden Street. The camel looks a good deal more at ease than the staff behind the bar!

All at sea. This photograph dates from before the Second World War. Cosens *Consul* then in her early days at Weymouth is probably on a charter trip. Flags flying, spectators on the stone pier and the number of naval ships in the Bay suggest this may have been the Review of the Fleet in August 1939.

CHAPTER SEVEN

OUT AND ABOUT

Scene changes

Standing at this spot today you would be looking at the late-twentieth-century housing development of The Maltings on the site of the Devenish brewery buildings in Rodwell Avenue. The decorative wrought iron sign has been preserved at the Brewer's Quay complex opposite.

Loading at the main brewery buildings in Hope Square. The Devenish and Groves breweries merged in 1960, the year that these photographs were taken. When Devenish ceased brewing in the town in the 1980s the redundant Hope Square building was converted to become Brewer's Quay incorporating 'The Timewalk', a special-effects journey through history, Weymouth Museum and a shopping village.

Netherton House at the Boot Hill junction of Rodwell Road and Chickerell Road is named on old maps as the Manor House and was obviously built for a person of some importance in 'old' Weymouth, set a little away from the bustling harbourside. Much of the building dates from the early-eighteenth century but there are indications of a much earlier structure within. 'The Netherton' was a hotel for many years and latterly a nursing home. The old wall shown extending up Boot Hill in 1969 has gone now. Houses were built along here in the 1990s.

Springfield House built of Portland stone for the Devenish family in 1879 (various Devenish motifs decorated the front of the building). Major J.H.C. Devenish died in 1953, intending by his Will that the house should be converted to provide homes for forces and clergy widows. This proved uneconomic and Springfield had been bomb-damaged in a 1942 air raid. It was sold to developers and pulled down. Houses in Portwey Close stand on part of the site, and bungalows in accordance with the terms of the Major's Will occupy the rest. More 'Devenish' homes were built in other areas of the borough.

Glebe House stood in Cross Road and was once Holy Trinity Church vicarage. A vicarage had already been partially built in Longfield Road in the 1850s but funds ran out and it was sold. A late-nineteenth-century incumbent found himself with enough money, thanks to a large donation made 'for the benefit of some poor parish', to build this fine vicarage, Glebe House, in Cross Road. Later parish priests found it too far from the church and moved back to Longfield Road. Like so many Victorian mansions, the house was set in the middle of extensive grounds – valuable building land for twentieth-century developers. It proved more profitable to raze the vicarage than convert it and the houses of Rectory Way and Glebe Close now fill the site.

Faircross House, seen here in 1957. It was built in the 1880s for local jeweller John Vincent and so named because an ancient Fair Cross had recently been found nearby. Vincent displayed the cross in the grounds of his house, which was demolished in 1973. The old cross now stands in front of the flats built on the site, off Faircross Avenue. Mr and Mrs Vincent lost their lives in the St Lawrence Seaway disaster of 1914 when the liner *Empress of Ireland* sank following a collision, drowning more than 1000 on board. The Vincents had been homeward-bound after visiting relations in Canada.

So tiny, yet so attractive in the street scene. These four cottages on the corner of Wyke Road and Gypsy Lane were built in 1829 to house 'four poor widows' of the borough. They survived until 1958 and were replaced by four modern bungalows in Rodwell Avenue. The site has since been redeveloped. The Georgian house in the background still stands.

Portwey Hospital, built in 1836, was originally the Weymouth Workhouse. Converted to serve as an emergency hospital in the Second World War, it is best remembered as a Maternity Hospital. This closed in 1987 and the building's subsequent conversion to housing has retained the impressive 'workhouse' façade almost unchanged. The photograph was taken in 1983.

Two embankment bridges took the Weymouth and Portland Railway line over roads in the town. The bridge at Pye Hill remains today and traffic lights have been installed to regulate traffic at this very narrow spot. The keystone was laid on the wedding day of the Prince of Wales (later Edward VII) in 1863 and is carved with the Prince of Wales feathers to commemorate the occasion. The Railway Arch Hotel has closed since these pictures were taken in 1965.

The second bridge, over Newstead Road, is no more. It was demolished in 1987 when road-widening was carried out here.

A number of new churches have been built in Weymouth in post-war years. This one, Newstead Road Methodist Chapel, replaced one on the same site destroyed by enemy bombs on 2 April 1942, a vicious dive-bombing raid which brought widespread damage to the town. The new chapel opened in April 1955.

The late-1960s saw the expansion of the council's housing estate at Westham. These houses were going up at Wiltshire Avenue, off Norfolk Road, in April 1968.

The development of sports facilities at The Marsh began soon after the First World War. At the time it was announced that the area would be known as Westham Playing Fields but the old name had been in common usage too long and 'The Marsh' it remained. This 1964 view shows the new Youth Activities Centre. Knightsdale Road is on the right. A further development in the area was the swimming pool, opened in 1974.

In the years since the Second World War some 15 schools have been built in and around Weymouth – some replacing outdated and outgrown premises, others for the new communities growing up outside the town area. Too many to include them all; three of the new schools are shown here. Weymouth Grammar School moved from Alma Road to Charlestown in the mid-1960s. Now known as Budmouth Technology College, additional buildings are currently going up alongside those shown here. The former W.G.S. buildings at Westham, taken over by South Dorset Technical College (later Weymouth College) now await demolition.

The growing population of Littlemoor saw its first school opened in 1961, here with one of the original classes of children.

The 'Rainbow School' at Wyke Regis (Wyke Regis County Infants School) – an innovative design by local architect E.Wamsley Lewis – opened on Portland Road in 1952. The sculpture outside was by local artist Eric Morris.

South Dorset Technical College, Newstead Road in 1961. The College opened here in 1939 and took over adjacent Weymouth Grammar School buildings when the school relocated to Charlestown in the late-1960s. A new College block was added in the 1970s. Now all the Newstead Road site is empty and awaits demolition. The College – since 1985 'Weymouth College' – operated on two sites, the second at Cranford Avenue. This latter site was expanded in 2000/1 to include all departments. Newstead Road will be developed as housing.

A South Dorset Technical College secretarial class in the pre-computer era, 1961.

Huge holes appeared in the landscape and faint underground rumblings were heard in the early-1980s as the construction of a new sewerage system took a tunnel under the hill separating Weymouth and Wyke Regis to a new treatment works west of Wyke village.

This stark view of the newly constructed main pumping station alongside Radipole Lake in 1982 is now softened by the growth of trees and shrubs. Weymouth Way passes in front of the building. On the higher ground above, Weymouth College buildings will disappear in 2001.

Underbarn and the steps leading down to Sandsfoot Cove. Landslips in this area result in the frequent closure of the cliff walk east of the cove. The 'wreck' is the centre of this 1959 photograph is actually an old torpedo testing target washed up and left on the beach. There is rather less of it forty years on but it is still there!

Sandesfort House, at the junction of Buxton Road and Rylands Lane. A private house from its building until after the Second World War when it became a Children's Home and, in the 1950s, Thornlow Senior School. The school closed in 1998. Houses will fill its grounds but the future of Sandesfort House is to be decided.

New street lighting at Foord's Corner, Wyke Regis, December 1960.

Wyke House, to the south of Chamberlaine Road, Wyke Regis. An imposing house in extensive grounds, dating from the late-eighteenth/early-nineteenth century. At the time the photograph was taken – 1966 – it was the Wyke House Hotel. The building was demolished in 1974 and the houses of Wooland Gardens now fill the site.

Ferrybridge in 1975. Soon concerns were to be expressed over the safety of the 1890s bridge, carrying heavy traffic to Portland and found to be rusting out. Passage over the bridge was restricted to single file and several years of long delays followed. Work on a new bridge included the cutting of a new channel closer to the island, diverting the Fleet waters. When the new bridge was completed in 1984 the channel shown here under the old bridge was filled in. In the background (right) are the buildings of the old Whitehead Torpedo Factory. These disappeared completely in 1997 and the houses of 'Harbour Point' now overlook Portland Harbour.

This 1935 photograph shows a local monument which can only be viewed close-up if you tramp the shingle of Chesil Beach. It is the Portland Bound Stone, restored that year, establishing the bounds of the Royal Manor of Portland. It stands almost opposite Lanehouse and every seven years the traditional 'Beating the Bounds' ceremony takes place here.

The Peto Memorial Reading Room at Chickerell was sadly derelict in 1972. Already dilapidated it had been further damaged by fire. Dorset County Council took it on and restored the building to its attractive former state, opening it as the village library in 1973, the purpose it still serves today. Fittingly, since the terms of Sir Henry Peto's donation to the village in 1890 stated that the rooms were to be used '...for reading, conversation, recreation and good fellowship and for such purposes in harmony therewith...'

An almost panoramic view as these two photographs take us 'down over Lanehouse' as Lanehouse Rocks Road descends the hill in 1956. Some distant fields have since been built over – by houses, schools and industrial estates.

Another scene change. This was the Compton Lodge Hotel with its two-storey extension in 1960. The site, adjacent to Weymouth Police Station in Dorchester Road, is now filled with a modern apartment block.

The 1909 Convent of the Sacred Hearts School in Carlton Road closed in 1992. It has been converted to apartments and houses have been built on the school's hockey field.

Tollhouses can still be seen on many country roads – relics of the turnpike trust days when funds to maintain the roads were raised by tolls levied on their users. This one, on Dorchester Road, stood almost opposite the Spa at Radipole, replacing an earlier one closer to the town in about 1840. Redundant at the end of the nineteenth century when county councils took over the upkeep of main and toll roads, it was converted into two cottages. It outlived its companion tollhouse on Preston Beach Road by some seventeen years but in 1976, it too succumbed to the bulldozer.

A busy scene at Radipole Laundry in 1960. It stood on the corner of Queens Road and Spa Road, closing in the late-1970s. An apartment block, Jubilee Court, now stands on the site. There had been an earlier laundry here – it burned down in 1910, a huge conflagration in the early hours which most of the residents of Radipole turned out to watch.

The little village school at Radipole, standing in such a picturesque setting opposite St Ann's Church and the Old Manor House. The photograph dates from 1957 – the school closed in 1972 when Radipole County Primary School opened in Manor Road.

The suburb of Southill developed extensively in the 1950s with the growth of the Southill and Calverley Estates. This view shows the new road across Radipole Lake in 1962 leading up to Field Barn Drive. Chafey's Avenue is on the left.

A Calverley Show House at Southill…

… and its interior. Light, spacious and furnished in contemporary style, featuring the new Scandinavian-style spindle-legged furniture and fashionable basket-style chair.

Amenities were needed by the expanding population of Southill and this shopping centre off Radipole Lane went up in 1974/5.

Today indistinguishable from other residential buildings in Dorchester Road, this was once the Railway Station Hotel at Broadwey. The erection of its new pub sign in the 1950s led to some lively correspondence in the local press – railway purists claiming that some small details of the scene – depicting the first train from Weymouth – were inaccurate. It was, nevertheless, a most attractive example of the signwriter's art.

Forty-five years ago fox-hunting was not the contentious issue it is today and spectators at the Cattistock Hunt Meeting at Upwey in March 1956 display no concern at the purpose of the assembly, although there were headline complaints in the local press when hounds stormed through private gardens in pursuit of their quarry.

A bleak view of Lodmoor in the 1950s when nobody really knew what to do with this vast watery expanse. Proposals over three decades included various 'holiday village' plans (the most ambitious being that of Sir Billy Butlin who planned a luxury holiday camp here in 1963) and a marina complex, none of which materialised. Eventually decisions were taken and today Lodmoor is a country park and nature reserve with compatible attractions such as the Sea Life Centre. Just behind the beach wall on the left of the picture can be seen the old tollhouse, known locally as 'Sugar-em Shorey's' after the Shorey family who resided there for many years. The tollhouse was demolished in 1959.

Standing in splendid isolation in what would become Brackendown Avenue is the White House in 1954. Today the whole of the open land in the foreground and the slopes of the hill right down to Lodmoor are filled with houses.

When this photograph was taken in 1951 the gardens in the foreground belonged to the Embassy Hotel, now renamed the Spyglass at Bowleaze. The coastguard cottages beyond (they can also be seen in the previous picture) are now less in number. Coastal erosion caused those at the end of the terrace to fall into the sea.

A walk along the old Preston Beach Wall had to be undertaken with care as there was a considerable drop down to the road in places. The then isolated 'White House' is on the left.

'Caravan Holidays here to stay' ran the *Dorset Daily Echo* headline in 1953. Post-war holidaymakers enjoyed the freedom of being able to come and go as they liked, freed from the restrictions of set meal times of a 'B and B'. This is Manor Farm Camp, Preston. Even in the Fifties concern was being expressed at the sudden spread of caravans over the town's outlying green fields.

Littlesea Camp in the 1960s.

The building of the crescent-shaped Riviera Hotel in 1937 bankrupted its original owner. It accommodated disabled evacuee children during the Second World War and eventually became part of Fred Pontin's holiday camp empire. In 1997 the reinforced concrete art-deco hotel was listed as a Grade II building of special architectural interest by the Department of National Heritage. Under new ownership, it was extensively refurbished in 2000. This photograph of Bowleaze Cove dates from 1961.

Demolition or restoration? Fortunately the decision in the 1950s was to restore these tumbledown cottages overlooking the pond at Sutton Poyntz. Today this is one of the most picturesque spots in the borough.

The White Horse of Osmington Hill. The chalk cutting commemorates the visits to Weymouth of King George III and depicts the 'Farmer King' horseback riding in the Dorset countryside of which he was so fond. To maintain the crisp outline and bright contrast the horse and his royal rider have to be periodically cleaned and weeded. During the Second World War attempts were made (not altogether successfully) to camouflage the pair with green canvas and thus deter enemy bombers.

Across the Bay from Weymouth, these two enormous radio dishes, visible for miles around, dominated the coast at Ringstead. They were erected in the 1950s but became redundant in 1973 when the U.S.A.F. base they served was closed. The dishes were dismantled in 1975.